Trace and color the shape. Trace the name.

square

square

CD-104333

Trace the squares. Count the squares. There are ___ squares. Color the squares.

CD-104333

Color the large squares blue. Color the small squares green.

Count the squares. There are ____ squares. Color the squares.

CD-104333

© Carson-Dellosa

Trace and color the shape. Trace and write the name.

circle

circle

Trace the circle in the flower. Draw another flower. Color the flowers.

CD-104333

Draw lines to connect the circles that are the same size.

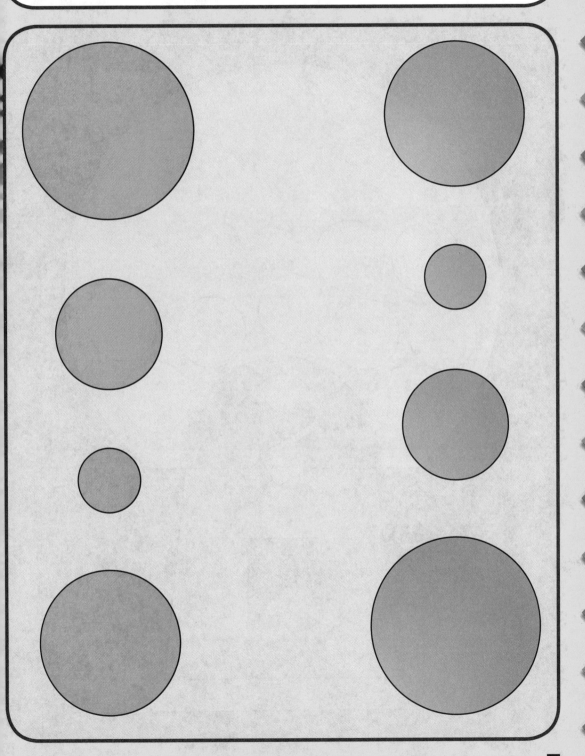

Count the circles. There are ____ circles. Color the circles.

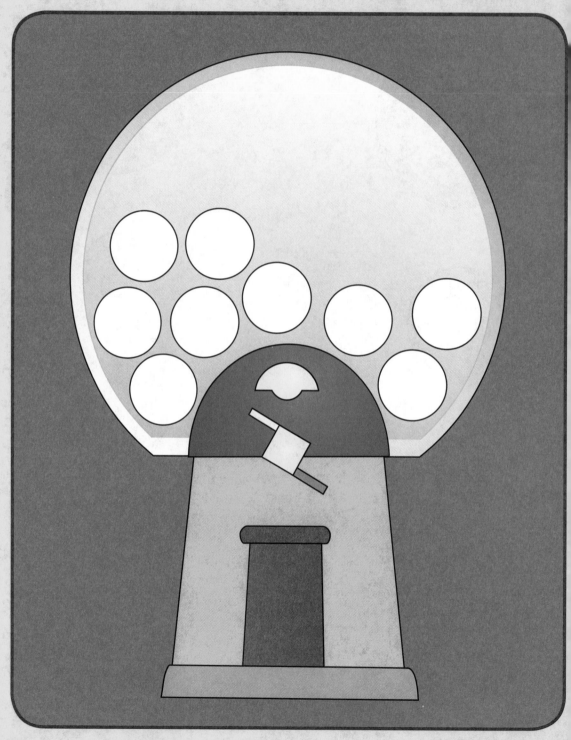

CD-104333

Color the squares brown. Color the circles orange.

Trace and color the shape. Trace and write the name.

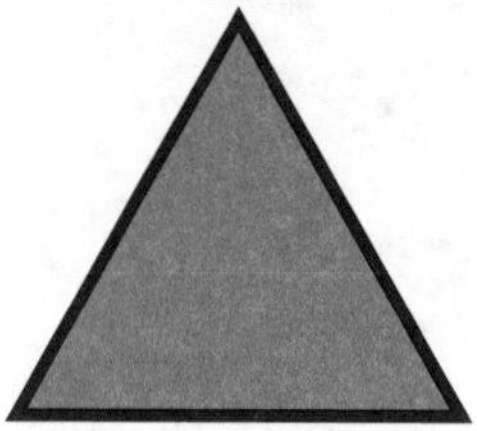

triangle

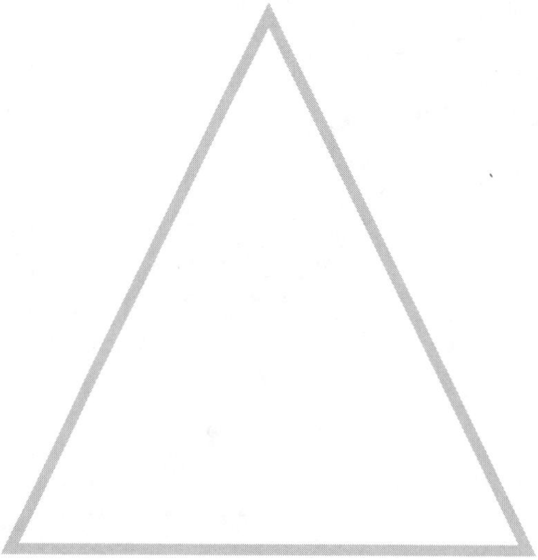

triangle

CD-104333

Trace the triangle in the ice-cream cone. Draw another ice-cream cone. Color the ice-cream cones.

CD-104333

11

Draw lines to connect the triangles that are the same size.

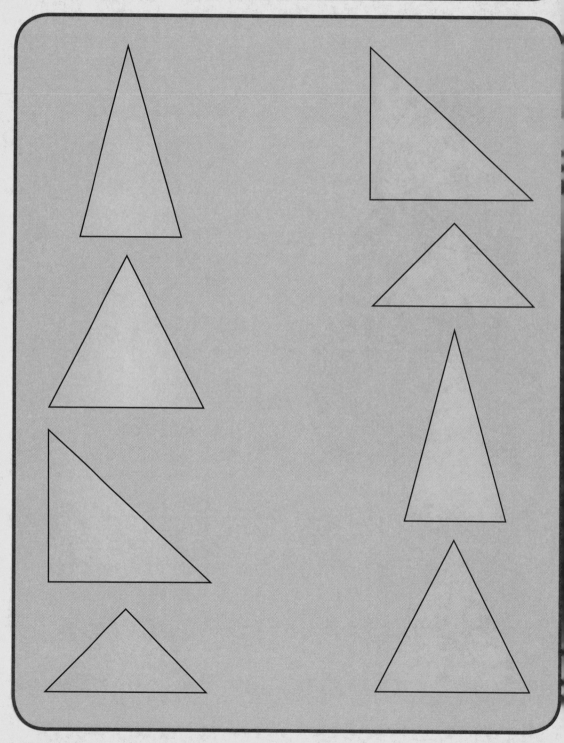

CD-104333

Count the triangles. There are ____ triangles. Color the triangles.

CD-104333

13

Color the triangles red. Color the circles green.

CD-104333

Color the squares to help the girl find the butterfly.

Start

Finish

Trace and color the shape. Trace and write the name.

rectangle

rectangle

CD-104333

Trace and color the rectangles.

Color the large rectangles blue. Color the small rectangles yellow.

CD-104333 © Carson-Dellosa

Count the rectangles. There are ___ rectangles. Color the rectangles.

Color the squares blue. Color the rectangles yellow.

CD-104333

Use the key to color the shapes.

square = blue   triangle = pink

circle = orange   rectangle = red

rhombus

rhombus

CD-104333 © Carson-Dellosa

Trace and color the rhombuses.

Color the large rhombuses purple. Color the small rhombuses green.

CD-104333

Count the rhombuses. There are ___ rhombuses. Color the rhombuses.

Color the triangles red. Color the rhombuses orange.

 CD-104333

Color the rectangles blue. Color the rhombuses red. Color the circles green. Color the squares purple.

CD-104333

27

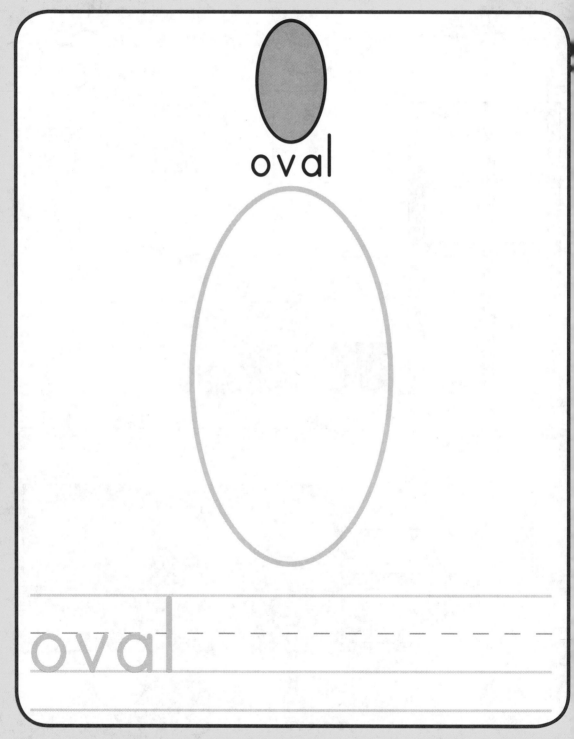

oval

oval

Trace the ovals. Draw another egg in the nest. Color the nest.

CD-104333

29

Color the large ovals red. Color the small ovals yellow.

CD-104333 © Carson-Dellosa

Count the ovals. There are ____ ovals. Color the ovals.

CD-104333 **31**

Color the ovals to help the hen find her eggs.

Start

Finish

Color the ovals purple. Color the rhombuses red.

CD-104333 **33**

Trace the shapes in each box. Color the pictures.

CD-104333

Use the key to color the shapes.

Color the square red. Color the rectangle blue. Color the circle purple. Color the triangle yellow.

CD-104333 © Carson-Dellosa

Count the triangles. There are ___ triangles.

CD-104333 **37**

Draw a line through the triangles to help the driver finish the race.

Start

Finish

Count the triangles in each flower. Write the number of triangles on the flowerpot.

CD-104333

39

Use the key to color the shapes.

square = green   triangle = blue
circle = orange   rectangle = yellow

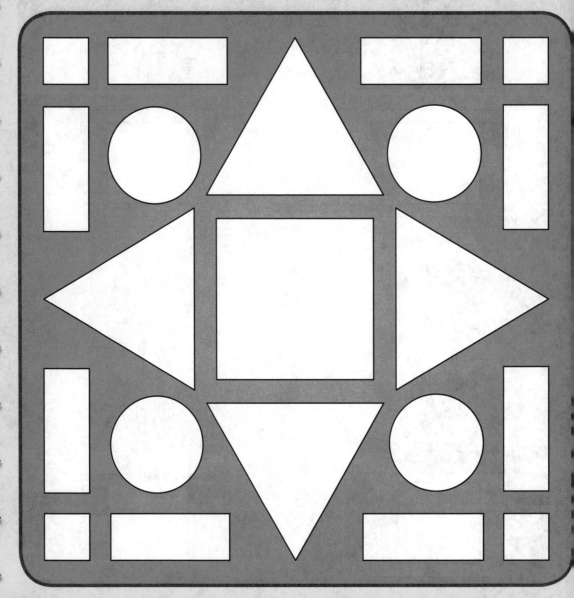

CD-104333

Use the key to color the shapes.

△ = blue   ◊ = brown   ▭ = purple

▢ = yellow   ◯ = red

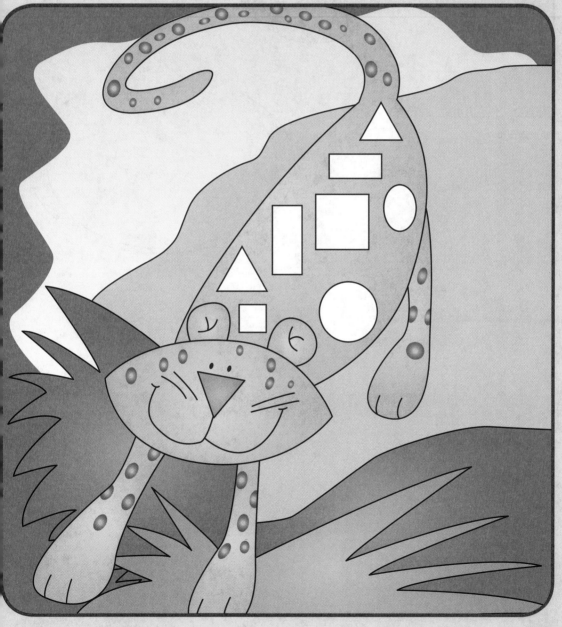

CD-104333   **41**

Trace the circles. Draw another planet. Color the picture.

 CD-104333

Count the triangles and circles. There are ____ triangles. There are ____ circles.

Count the ovals and circles. There are ____ ovals. There are ____ circles.

CD-104333 © Carson-Dellosa

Color the ovals pink. Color the circles yellow. Color the triangles green.

CD-104333

45

Trace the shapes. Color the shapes.

CD-104333 © Carson-Dellosa

Color the circles to help the astronaut find the spaceship.

Start

Finish

Trace the shapes.

CD-104333 © Carson-Dellosa

Use the key to color the shapes.

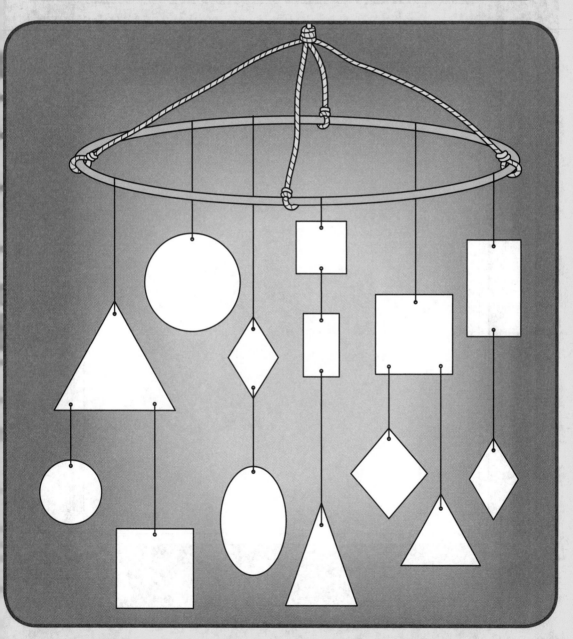

Draw a house using the shapes that you have learned.

CD-104333 © Carson-Dellosa

Draw animals using the shapes. The first animal has been drawn for you.

Draw a picture using I circle, I rectangle, 2 squares, and 2 triangles.

CD-I04333

Draw a face in each shape.

CD-104333 **53**

Draw lines to connect the shapes that are the same.

CD-104333 © Carson-Dellosa

Color the matching shapes the same color.

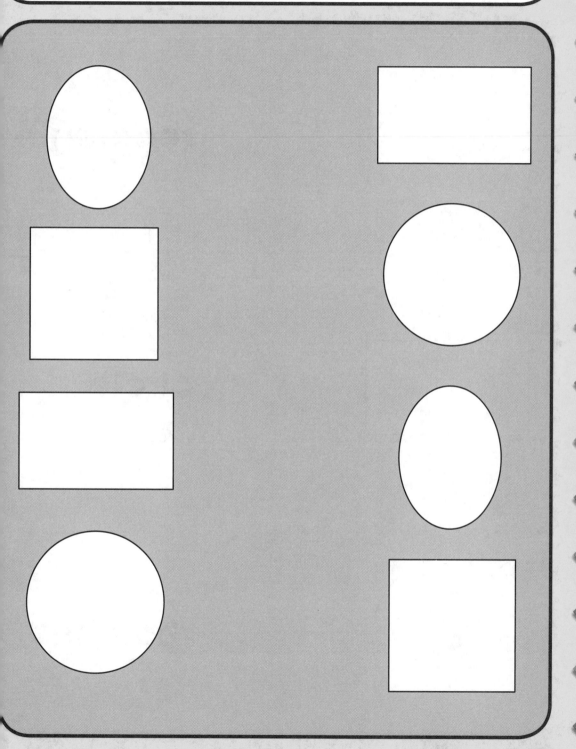

CD-104333 **55**

Draw a line to match each shape to the correct name. Color the shapes.

rectangle

circle

rhombus

CD-104333

Draw a line to match each shape to the correct name. Color the shapes.

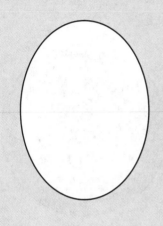

square

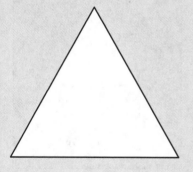

oval

triangle

 CD-104333

Draw a line to match each object to the correct shape.

CD-104333

Draw a line to match each object to the correct shape.

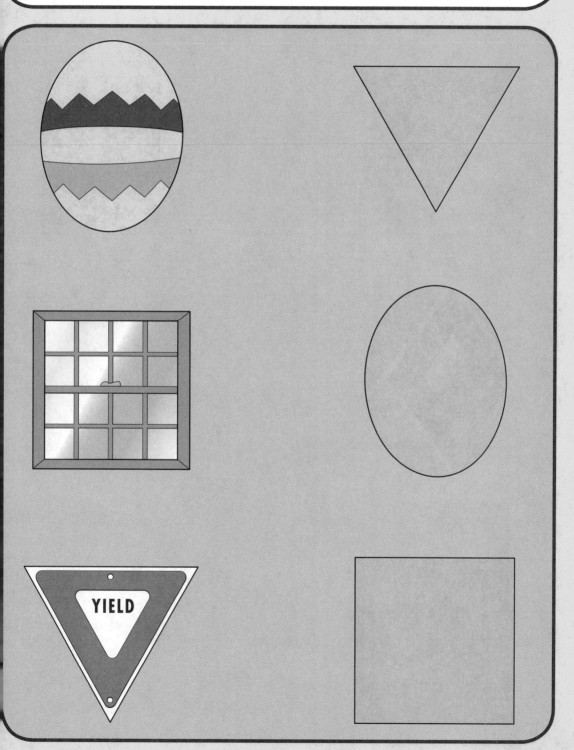

Draw a line to match each object to the correct shape.

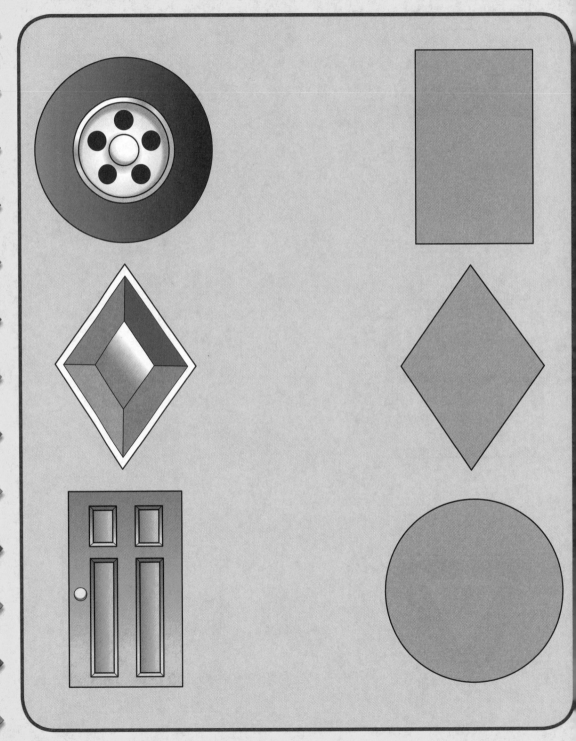

CD-104333 © Carson-Dellosa

Draw a line to match each object to the correct shape.

Circle the squares and rectangles. Draw squares around the ovals and circles. Draw Xs on the triangles and rhombuses.

CD-104333 © Carson-Dellosa

Find the shapes hidden in the picture. Use the key to color the shapes.

☐ = yellow	△ = red	◯ = green	
◯ = purple	▭ = orange	◇ = blue	

Watermelons $1.25

Beans Beans Beans Beans

Soup

Bananas

Use the key to complete the sentence.

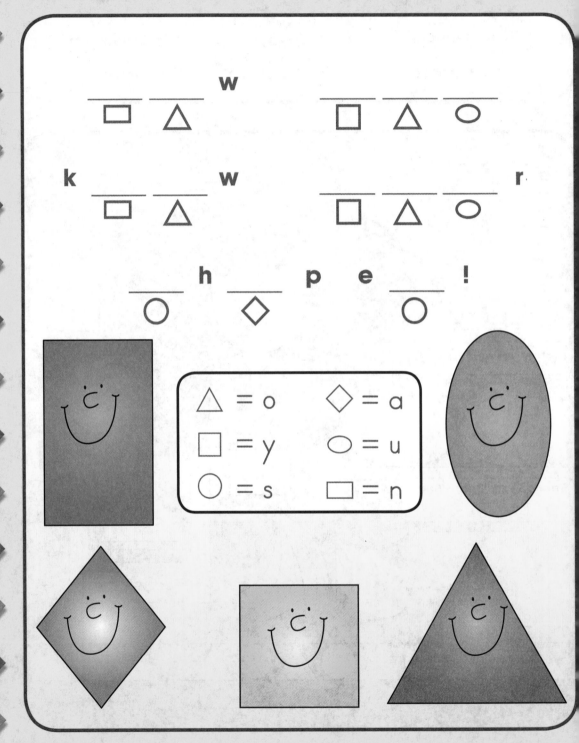

Key:
△ = o   ◇ = a
□ = y   ⬭ = u
○ = s   ▭ = n

CD-104333